52-WEEK

DEVOTIONAL

FOR DADS

Published by Midsummer Bloom Books

First Edition: September 2025
Printed in the United States of America

CONTENTS

INTRODUCTION

Welcome, dad. You picked up this book because you want to be the father God has called you to be. That takes courage. Being a dad in today's world isn't easy—you're pulled in countless directions, wrestling with doubts, facing pressures your own father may never have known.

But here's what I want you to know: God sees you. He knows every sacrifice you make, every prayer you whisper over sleeping children, every moment you choose patience when you're running on empty. He hasn't just called you to be a father; He's equipped you for it.

This devotional isn't about adding more to your plate. It's about finding God in the beautiful chaos of fatherhood. Each week, you'll discover truths from Scripture that speak directly to your journey as a dad. You'll find prayers to strengthen you, challenges to grow you, and moments to reconnect with the Father who loves you perfectly.

Some weeks you'll feel victorious. Others, you'll come broken and tired. Both are welcome here. God's grace meets you wherever you are.

Your kids don't need a perfect dad—they need a present one who's learning to lean on God. So let's walk this journey together, one week at a time, discovering how God transforms ordinary fathers into men who leave eternal legacies.

Your family is waiting for the dad God is shaping you to become. Let's begin.

WEEK 1: YOU ARE MORE THAN A PROVIDER

GOD'S TRUTH

"For we are his workmanship, created in Christ Jesus for good works, which God prepared beforehand, that we should walk in them."–
Ephesians 2:10 (ESV)

DEVOTIONAL THOUGHT

You work hard to put food on the table, keep a roof overhead, and meet your family's needs. That provider instinct runs deep, and it's good. But somewhere along the way, the world convinced you that your paycheck defines your worth as a father. That lie has crushed too many good men.

God's truth cuts through that deception. You are His workmanship—His masterpiece. Before you were a provider, you were purposefully crafted by the Creator of the universe. Your value isn't measured in dollars earned or hours worked. It's measured by the God who formed you with intention and love.

Your kids need more than what money can buy. They need your presence, your wisdom, your laughter, and your prayers. They need to see you fail and get back up. They need to watch you worship, serve, and love their mother well. These are the good works God prepared for you long before you held your first child.

Yes, providing matters. But you're also a teacher, protector, encourager, and spiritual leader. You're the one who shows them what God's love looks like with skin on. When you embrace this fuller picture of fatherhood, you step into the purpose God designed specifically for you.

A PRAYER FOR YOU

Father, help me see myself through Your eyes, not the world's. When I feel reduced to just a paycheck, remind me I'm Your workmanship. Give me wisdom to provide not just financially, but emotionally and spiritually for my family. Show me the good works You've prepared for me today. Amen.

YOUR CHALLENGE

This week, spend fifteen minutes each day doing something with your kids that costs nothing but means everything—throw a ball, read a story, or just listen to their day. Notice how their faces light up when you give them your undivided attention. That's you being more than a provider; that's you being Dad.

TAKE A MOMENT

Stand in your children's doorway tonight while they sleep. Watch them breathe. Think about all the ways you matter to them beyond what you provide financially. Let that truth sink deep into your heart.

WEEK 2: GOD'S STRENGTH FOR FATHERHOOD

GOD'S TRUTH

"But he said to me, 'My grace is sufficient for you, for my power is made perfect in weakness.' Therefore I will boast all the more gladly of my weaknesses, so that the power of Christ may rest upon me."–2 Corinthians 12:9 (ESV)

DEVOTIONAL THOUGHT

Every dad knows that three-in-the-morning feeling when the baby won't stop crying, you have a presentation at eight, and you're running on fumes. Or when your teenager slams the door, and you have no idea how to bridge the gap. Fatherhood has a way of exposing every weakness you thought you'd hidden.

Here's the liberating truth: God isn't disappointed by your weakness. He's actually drawn to it. When Paul begged God to remove his struggle, God revealed something revolutionary—divine power shows up best in human weakness. Your limitations aren't liabilities; they're invitations for God's strength.

That moment when you don't know what to say to your hurting child? God's wisdom is available. When anger rises and you're about to explode? His patience can flow through you. When you're too exhausted to read one more bedtime story? His strength can carry you.

Stop trying to be a superhero dad. Your kids don't need you to have it all together. They need to see you depending on Someone greater than yourself. When they watch you pray through problems, lean on God's Word, and admit your need for grace, they learn that real strength comes from above. Your weakness becomes the stage where God's power performs its greatest work.

A PRAYER FOR YOU

Lord, I'm tired of pretending I'm stronger than I am. Thank You that Your grace is enough for every parenting challenge I face. When I'm weak, be my strength. Let Your power rest on me today, especially in the moments when I have nothing left to give. Amen.

YOUR CHALLENGE

Identify your biggest weakness as a father—patience, consistency, emotional availability, whatever it is. Each morning this week, specifically ask God to be strong in that exact area. Watch how He shows up in unexpected ways when you stop hiding your weakness and start inviting His power.

TAKE A MOMENT

Find a quiet spot in your home and simply breathe. With each exhale, release the pressure to be the perfect dad. With each inhale, receive God's sufficient grace for this moment, this day, this season of fatherhood.

WEEK 3: LEADING WITH LOVE, NOT FEAR

GOD'S TRUTH

"There is no fear in love, but perfect love casts out fear. For fear has to do with punishment, and whoever fears has not been perfected in love."–1 John 4:18 (ESV)

DEVOTIONAL THOUGHT

Maybe you grew up in a home where Dad's word was law, enforced by fear. "Wait till your father gets home" sent shivers down your spine. Or perhaps you swing the opposite way, afraid to discipline at all. Either extreme misses God's heart for fatherhood.

God shows us a better way—leading with love that casts out fear. This doesn't mean being a pushover. It means your children obey not because they're terrified of consequences, but because they trust your love for them. They know that behind every boundary is a father who'd take a bullet for them.

When you lead with love, correction comes wrapped in affection. Your kids learn that discipline isn't Dad losing control; it's Dad loving them too much to let them wander into danger. They feel safe making mistakes because they know your love isn't conditional on their performance.

Fear-based parenting produces anxious kids who either rebel or perform for approval. Love-based leadership raises secure children who understand boundaries exist because they're treasured. When your kids know deep in their bones that Dad's love is unshakeable, they're free to grow, fail, learn, and become who God created them to be. That's the power of perfect love—it drives out fear and creates space for real relationship.

A PRAYER FOR YOU

Father, forgive me for the times I've led with fear or anger instead of love. Fill me with Your perfect love that casts out fear. Help me discipline with wisdom and affection, showing my children that my love for them is as unchangeable as Yours is for me. Amen.

YOUR CHALLENGE

Before any correction this week, pause and ask yourself: "Am I responding from love or reacting from frustration?" Take a breath, remember God's patient love for you, then address the situation. Notice how this shift changes both your approach and your child's response to discipline.

TAKE A MOMENT

Picture your child's face when they've disappointed you. Now imagine God looking at you with that same perfect love when you've failed. Let that divine perspective reshape how you'll lead your family today.

WEEK 4: WHEN YOU FEEL LIKE YOU'RE NOT ENOUGH

GOD'S TRUTH

"And God is able to make all grace abound to you, so that having all sufficiency in all things at all times, you may abound in every good work."–2 Corinthians 9:8 (ESV)

DEVOTIONAL THOUGHT

The comparison trap is real. You scroll through social media seeing other dads coaching three sports, building treehouses, and taking exotic family vacations. Meanwhile, you're just trying to survive Tuesday. That voice whispers, "You're not enough. Your kids deserve better."

Stop right there. God doesn't call you to be that other dad. He called you to be your children's father. And here's the promise: His grace is abundant enough to equip you for exactly what your family needs. Not what the Jones family needs. Yours.

Maybe you can't afford Disney World, but you tell the best bedtime stories. Perhaps you're not handy with tools, but you never miss a recital. You might work long hours, but your kids know Dad prays for them every single day. God's sufficiency shows up in your unique situation.

The enemy wants you paralyzed by inadequacy, but God says you have all sufficiency in all things at all times. That's not motivational fluff—it's divine promise. Every good work

He's called you to as a father, He's already equipped you to accomplish. Your kids don't need a perfect dad. They need the dad God specifically chose for them. That's you, inadequacies and all.

A PRAYER FOR YOU

Lord, silence the voices telling me I'm not enough. Help me trust that Your grace is sufficient for every fathering challenge I face. Show me that You've already equipped me with everything I need to be the dad my children need today. Thank You for choosing me for them. Amen.

YOUR CHALLENGE

Write down three things you do well as a father—things unique to you. Maybe it's your humor, your steadiness, or your willingness to apologize. This week, lean into those strengths instead of obsessing over what you lack. God gave you those specific gifts for your specific kids.

TAKE A MOMENT

Look at a photo of your children. Remember the day they were born and how God entrusted them specifically to you. He didn't make a mistake. You are exactly the father they need.

WEEK 5: BUILDING A LEGACY OF FAITH

GOD'S TRUTH

"One generation shall commend your works to another, and shall declare your mighty acts."–Psalm 145:4 (ESV)

DEVOTIONAL THOUGHT

What will your kids remember about Dad's faith? Not the perfect Sunday attendance or the memorized verses, but the authentic moments when they caught you depending on God. Legacy isn't built in grand gestures; it's constructed one ordinary day at a time.

Your children are watching when you pray over bills that seem impossible. They notice when you choose forgiveness instead of bitterness. They see you reading your Bible at the kitchen table before the sun rises. These unscripted moments are writing the story of faith they'll tell their own children someday.

Building a spiritual legacy doesn't require theological degrees or perfect answers to every question. It requires showing up consistently with authentic faith. When you admit you don't have all the answers but you know Who does, you're teaching them to trust God, not just Dad.

The faith you're passing down isn't just information about God—it's an introduction to Him. Your kids learn to hear His voice by watching you listen. They learn to trust His promises by seeing you stand on them during storms. Every prayer, every act of worship, every moment of surrender is a brick in the legacy you're building. Generations you'll never meet will be impacted by the faith you live out today.

A PRAYER FOR YOU

Father, help me build a legacy that points to You. Make my faith so real and authentic that my children can't help but want to know You personally. Use my ordinary obedience to impact generations I'll never meet. Let my life declare Your mighty acts. Amen.

YOUR CHALLENGE

Start one simple faith tradition this week that your kids will remember—pray before meals if you don't already, share one thing you're grateful to God for at bedtime, or play worship music during Saturday morning pancakes. Consistency matters more than complexity. Pick something sustainable and stick with it.

TAKE A MOMENT

Imagine your grandchildren or great-grandchildren hearing stories about you. What do you hope they'll hear about your faith? Let that vision inspire how you'll live out your faith in front of your kids today.

WEEK 6: FINDING JOY IN BEING A DAD

GOD'S TRUTH

"You make known to me the path of life; in your presence there is fullness of joy; at your right hand are pleasures forevermore."–Psalm 16:11 (ESV)

DEVOTIONAL THOUGHT

Somewhere between sleepless nights, teenage attitudes, and endless responsibilities, joy can feel like a luxury you can't afford. You love your kids fiercely, but honestly? Some days feel more like survival than celebration. If guilt just stabbed you for thinking that, you're not alone.

Here's what changes everything: joy isn't found in perfect circumstances but in God's presence. And guess what? He's right there in the chaos with you. In the middle of meltdowns and messes, His presence offers fullness of joy—not because everything's perfect, but because He's with you.

Joy looks different in fatherhood. It's your toddler's belly laugh at your silly face. It's your teenager actually talking to you about their day. It's watching your child show kindness to someone else. These moments are God whispering, "This is the path of life I'm showing you."

The enemy wants to steal your joy by keeping your eyes on the frustrations. But when you look for God's presence in your fathering journey, joy surprises you. It shows up in bedtime prayers, family dance parties, and even in the teachable moments after mistakes. Your kids need to see that following God and being their dad brings you deep joy. That joy becomes contagious, filling your home with the atmosphere of heaven.

A PRAYER FOR YOU

Lord, forgive me for letting the weight of responsibility steal my joy. Help me find You in the beautiful chaos of fatherhood. Open my eyes to the daily gifts hidden in ordinary moments. Fill our home with the joy that comes from Your presence. Let my kids see that being their dad brings me joy. Amen.

YOUR CHALLENGE

Each day this week, intentionally create one moment of pure fun with your kids—have a pillow fight, tell jokes at dinner, dance to their favorite song. Don't wait for joy to find you; actively pursue it. Watch how these simple moments shift the atmosphere of your home.

TAKE A MOMENT

Recall your favorite memory with your kids from the past month. Sit with that memory for a full minute, thanking God for that glimpse of joy. Let gratitude reset your perspective on fatherhood.

WEEK 7: GRATITUDE THAT CHANGES YOUR PERSPECTIVE

GOD'S TRUTH

"Give thanks in all circumstances; for this is the will of God in Christ Jesus for you."–1 Thessalonians 5:18 (ESV)

DEVOTIONAL THOUGHT

It's easy to focus on what's going wrong. The defiant preschooler, the moody preteen, the bills that keep coming. Your mind naturally gravitates toward problems that need fixing. But what if gratitude could completely shift your perspective on fatherhood?

Paul doesn't say give thanks FOR all circumstances—that would be cruel. He says IN all circumstances. Even in the struggle, you can find something to thank God for. That strong-willed child? They'll be a world-changer. That teenager pushing boundaries? They're becoming independent. Those financial pressures? They're teaching your family to trust God together.

Gratitude isn't denial; it's choosing to see God's hand even in hard seasons. When you actively look for reasons to be thankful, something shifts. The same situations look different through grateful eyes. Your kids sense the change too. Instead of Dad always being stressed, they see Dad finding good even in difficult days.

This isn't fake positivity—it's spiritual warfare. The enemy wants you overwhelmed and defeated. But when you choose gratitude, you're declaring that God is still good, still working, still worthy of praise. Your thankful heart becomes a testimony to your children that circumstances don't determine joy. Watch how gratitude transforms not just your perspective, but the entire atmosphere of your home.

A PRAYER FOR YOU

Father, forgive my complaining heart. Help me see reasons for gratitude even in challenging seasons. Open my eyes to the gifts hidden in my daily life as a dad. Let my children see me choosing thankfulness, teaching them that You're worthy of praise in every circumstance. Amen.

YOUR CHALLENGE

Start each dinner this week by having everyone share one thing they're grateful for—you go first. Make it specific and genuine. On hard days, push through the resistance and find something. Notice how this simple practice shifts your family's focus from problems to blessings.

TAKE A MOMENT

Think of your most challenging child or situation right now. Find one thing about that challenge you can genuinely thank God for—even if it's just that He's using it to grow your patience. Let gratitude reframe your perspective.

WEEK 8: TRUSTING GOD WITH YOUR FAMILY'S FUTURE

GOD'S TRUTH

"For I know the plans I have for you, declares the Lord, plans for welfare and not for evil, to give you a future and a hope."–Jeremiah 29:11 (ESV)

DEVOTIONAL THOUGHT

The world feels increasingly uncertain. You watch the news and wonder what kind of future your kids will inherit. Will they find good jobs? Stay strong in faith? Be safe? The weight of their tomorrow can crush your peace today.

But God's promise stands firm: He has plans for your family, and they're good plans. Not maybe, not hopefully—definitely. The God who sees the end from the beginning has already walked through your children's future, preparing good works for them to walk in.

This doesn't mean life will be easy or pain-free. It means God's purposes will prevail. Every struggle your kids face is developing strength they'll need later. Every disappointment is teaching them to find hope in God, not circumstances. He's writing a story with their lives that's bigger than you can imagine.

Your job isn't to control their future—it's to trust the One who holds it. When you model that trust, your kids learn that uncertainty isn't scary when you know Who's in charge. They watch you hand over your parental anxieties to God and find peace. That's a gift more valuable than any college fund. Release the illusion of control. God's plans for your family are better than anything you could orchestrate.

A PRAYER FOR YOU

Lord, I release my grip on my family's future. Help me trust that Your plans for my children are good, even when I can't see the path. Give me peace about tomorrow and wisdom for today. Let my kids see me trusting You with their lives. Amen.

YOUR CHALLENGE

This week, when anxiety about your family's future rises, stop and pray specifically about that fear. Hand it to God out loud if needed. Then take one practical step you can control today—have a good conversation, teach a life skill, or simply be present. Focus on faithful today; let God handle tomorrow.

TAKE A MOMENT

Picture each of your children as adults. Imagine God's good plans unfolding in their lives. Thank Him in advance for the story He's writing, even though you can't see all the chapters yet.

WEEK 9: THE GIFT OF BEING FULLY PRESENT

GOD'S TRUTH

"Look carefully then how you walk, not as unwise but as wise, making the best use of the time, because the days are evil."—Ephesians 5:15-16 (ESV)

DEVOTIONAL THOUGHT

Your phone buzzes. Work emails pile up. The game's on TV. A thousand things compete for your attention while your six-year-old tugs at your sleeve, "Dad, watch this!" How many moments slip away while you're physically present but mentally elsewhere?

Time is the one resource you can't earn more of. These years with your kids at home are shockingly brief. The toddler wanting you to watch him jump off the couch becomes the teenager who barely speaks at dinner. The little girl begging for one more story becomes the young woman walking down the aisle.

Being present isn't just about time management—it's about wisdom. In a world designed to distract, choosing presence is spiritual warfare. Every moment you give your kids your full attention, you're declaring they matter more than any notification, deadline, or distraction.

Your kids can tell the difference between Dad being there and Dad being THERE. When you put down the phone, make eye contact, and enter their world completely, you're giving them something money can't buy—the gift of being known, heard, and valued. These focused moments become the memories they'll treasure long after you're gone. The days are evil, full of things stealing your attention. Fight back by being fully present.

A PRAYER FOR YOU

Father, forgive me for the moments I've missed while being distracted. Help me see the eternal value in being fully present with my kids. Give me wisdom to recognize what truly matters and the discipline to choose presence over productivity. Let my children feel truly seen and heard. Amen.

YOUR CHALLENGE

Create a daily "phone-free zone"—maybe dinner time or the hour before bed. Put your phone in another room, not just on silent. Use this time to be completely present with your family. Notice what you discover about your kids when you're fully available to see it.

TAKE A MOMENT

Sit quietly and think about your favorite memory with your own father or a father figure. Chances are, it wasn't expensive or elaborate—it was a moment when you had their full attention. Choose to give that same gift to your children today.

WEEK 10: TEACHING YOUR KIDS TO RELY ON GOD

GOD'S TRUTH

"Trust in the Lord with all your heart, and do not lean on your own understanding. In all your ways acknowledge him, and he will make straight your paths."–Proverbs 3:5-6 (ESV)

DEVOTIONAL THOUGHT

Your instinct is to fix everything for your kids. Scraped knee? You've got a bandage. Hurt feelings? You'll make it better. But what happens when they face problems you can't solve? The diagnosis you can't cure, the heartbreak you can't prevent, the path you can't clear?

The greatest gift you can give your children isn't solving all their problems—it's teaching them to trust the Problem Solver. When they see you turning to God's Word for wisdom, they learn where to find answers. When they watch you pray through difficulties instead of panic, they discover where real help comes from.

This means letting them see you NOT have all the answers sometimes. "I don't know, but let's ask God about it." Those words teach dependence on Him, not you. It means praying with them about their problems instead of just fixing everything. It means pointing them to Scripture when they're struggling.

You're raising them for a world you won't always be in. Someday they'll face storms without Dad beside them. But if you've taught them to lean on God, they'll never truly be alone. Every time you choose faith over fear in front of them, you're showing them how to trust God with their whole heart.

A PRAYER FOR YOU

Lord, help me point my children to You, not myself, as their ultimate source. Give me wisdom to know when to step back and let them learn to lean on You. Help me model trust that teaches them to acknowledge You in all their ways. Amen.

YOUR CHALLENGE

This week, when your child comes with a problem, try responding with, "Let's pray about that together" before jumping to solve it. Help them learn to bring their concerns to God first. Then work together on practical steps, showing them how faith and action work together.

TAKE A MOMENT

Remember a time when God came through for you in an impossible situation. Consider how you can share that story with your children in an age-appropriate way, helping them see that God is trustworthy.

WEEK 11: PROTECTING YOUR FAMILY WITH FAITH

GOD'S TRUTH

"The name of the Lord is a strong tower; the righteous run into it and are safe."–Proverbs 18:10 (ESV)

DEVOTIONAL THOUGHT

Every dad feels it—that primal urge to protect your family from every threat. You check locks, install car seats, review screen time. But some dangers can't be stopped by dead bolts or safety protocols. Anxiety, depression, spiritual attacks, cultural pressures—these enemies require different weapons.

The strongest protection you can provide isn't physical—it's spiritual. When you cover your family in prayer, you're building walls no enemy can breach. When you speak God's promises over your children, you're equipping them with armor for battles you won't see coming.

This doesn't mean neglecting practical safety. It means recognizing that your family's ultimate security comes from the Lord. His name is the strong tower where your loved ones find true safety. Your job is to constantly point them toward that tower, showing them how to run to God when life gets scary.

Every prayer you pray over sleeping children is a shield. Every scripture you teach them becomes a sword they'll wield later. When you lead your family in trusting God's protection, you're not being passive—you're engaging in the most active form of defense available. You're teaching them that no matter what comes, they have a refuge that never fails. That's protection that lasts beyond your lifetime.

A PRAYER FOR YOU

Father, I can't protect my family from everything, but You can. Cover my children with Your protection. Give me wisdom to guard them physically and spiritually. Help me teach them to run to You as their strong tower. Be their refuge when I can't be there. Amen.

YOUR CHALLENGE

Start praying protection over each family member by name every morning—even if it's just while you're in the shower or driving to work. Ask God to guard their hearts, minds, and bodies. Speak specific promises from Scripture over situations they're facing.

TAKE A MOMENT

Walk through your home tonight after everyone's asleep. In each room, quietly pray for God's protection over the person who sleeps there. Thank Him for being the strong tower your family can always run to.

WEEK 12: BALANCING WORK AND FATHERHOOD

GOD'S TRUTH

"Whatever you do, work heartily, as for the Lord and not for men, knowing that from the Lord you will receive the inheritance as your reward. You are serving the Lord Christ."–Colossians 3:23-24 (ESV)

DEVOTIONAL THOUGHT

The tension is real. Work demands excellence and long hours. Your family needs presence and attention. You feel torn between providing well and being present, between career advancement and bedtime stories. Some days it feels like you're failing at both.

Here's the perspective shift: both your work and your fatherhood are service to the Lord. That presentation at work? You're serving Christ. Reading to your kids? You're serving Christ. This isn't about balance as much as it's about bringing excellence and presence to whatever God has placed before you in each moment.

Sometimes work will demand more—that's reality. But your children need to know that even when Dad's working hard, they're the reason why. They need to hear that your job is how you serve God and serve them, but they matter more than any position or paycheck.

The key is intentionality. When you're at work, work heartily. When you're home, be home fully. Your kids would rather have thirty minutes of Dad's complete attention than three hours of Dad physically present but mentally at the office. God sees both your diligence at work and your devotion at home. Both honor Him when done with the right heart.

A PRAYER FOR YOU

Lord, help me see both work and fatherhood as ways to serve You. Give me wisdom to know when to push hard at work and when to close the laptop. Help my children know they're more important than any job, while understanding why I work hard. Guide me in honoring You in both arenas. Amen.

YOUR CHALLENGE

This week, create one clear boundary between work and family time—maybe no emails after 7 PM or no work calls during dinner. Stick to it. Explain to your kids why you're doing this, helping them see that they're worth protecting time for.

TAKE A MOMENT

Think about why you work as hard as you do. Beyond the paycheck, what drives you? Let that deeper purpose motivate excellence at work while also reminding you what truly matters when you walk through your front door.

WEEK 13: SEEING YOUR KIDS THROUGH GOD'S EYES

GOD'S TRUTH

"For you formed my inward parts; you knitted me together in my mother's womb. I praise you, for I am fearfully and wonderfully made."–Psalm 139:13-14 (ESV)

DEVOTIONAL THOUGHT

It's easy to see what your kids aren't. Not as athletic as you'd hoped. Not as academic as their sibling. Not as outgoing, compliant, or driven as you expected. When you focus on what's lacking, you miss the miracle right in front of you.

God knitted each of your children together with intentionality. That personality quirk that drives you crazy? God wired it into them for a purpose. The child who exhausts you with questions might be your future scientist. The one who argues everything could become a lawyer fighting for justice. God doesn't make mistakes.

When you see your kids through God's eyes, everything changes. Instead of trying to reshape them into your image, you help them discover who God created them to be. You celebrate their uniqueness instead of comparing them to others. You speak life into their differences instead of trying to sand down their edges.

Your words have incredible power. When you tell your child what God sees in them—their gifts, their potential, their value—you're agreeing with heaven's perspective. You become a mirror reflecting their true identity. Every child needs someone who sees them the way God does. That's your privilege as their dad. Look closer. See what God sees.

A PRAYER FOR YOU

Father, forgive me for the times I've wished my children were different. Open my eyes to see them as You do—fearfully and wonderfully made. Help me celebrate their uniqueness instead of trying to change it. Show me how to speak Your truth about who they are. Amen.

YOUR CHALLENGE

This week, identify one trait in each child that you've seen as a weakness. Ask God to show you how He might use that very trait for His purposes. Then encourage your child specifically about that characteristic, helping them see it as a strength in development.

TAKE A MOMENT

Study each of your children's faces when they're not aware you're watching. Thank God for the specific ways He's crafted them. Marvel at the intricate work He's done in creating these unique individuals entrusted to your care.

WEEK 14: LEADING YOUR FAMILY CLOSER TO GOD

GOD'S TRUTH

"As for me and my house, we will serve the Lord."–
Joshua 24:15 (ESV)

DEVOTIONAL THOUGHT

Joshua didn't say, "I hope my house will serve the Lord" or "I'll try to get my family interested in God." He made a declaration of leadership. As for me and my house—that's a father taking spiritual responsibility. The question isn't whether you'll lead your family spiritually, but where you'll lead them.

Every family follows something. Sports, success, comfort, entertainment—these become gods by default when Dad doesn't actively lead toward the true God. Your children are watching to see what really matters to you. Do they see faith as something Dad does on Sundays, or as the foundation of every decision?

Leading your family to God doesn't require perfection. It requires direction. When your kids see you reading Scripture, they learn God's Word matters. When problems arise and you pray first, they learn where help comes from. When you choose church over travel sports, they learn priorities.

You're the spiritual thermostat of your home, not the thermometer. You don't just reflect the spiritual temperature—you set it. This might feel overwhelming, but remember: God called you to this. He doesn't call the qualified; He qualifies the called. Every small step you take toward God, you take your family with you. That's the power and privilege of spiritual leadership.

A PRAYER FOR YOU

Lord, I declare that my house will serve You. Give me courage to lead spiritually, even when I feel inadequate. Help me set a spiritual temperature in our home that draws my family closer to You. Show me practical ways to point them to You daily. Amen.

YOUR CHALLENGE

This week, initiate one spiritual conversation or activity you've been avoiding—maybe family devotions, prayer before bed, or discussing Sunday's sermon at dinner. Don't wait to feel ready. Take the first step and watch God honor your obedience as you lead your family closer to Him.

TAKE A MOMENT

Envision your family actively serving and loving God together five years from now. What would that look like? Let that vision motivate the spiritual leadership decisions you make today.

WEEK 15: TACKLING STRESS WITH GOD'S POWER

GOD'S TRUTH

"Cast all your anxiety on him because he cares for you."–1 Peter 5:7 (ESV)

DEVOTIONAL THOUGHT

The stress inventory keeps growing. Mortgage payments, job pressures, marriage tensions, kid problems—they pile up like unpaid bills. You feel the weight physically. Shoulders tight, jaw clenched, lying awake at three AM with your mind racing through worst-case scenarios. Your family feels it too, walking on eggshells around stressed-out Dad.

Peter doesn't suggest you might want to consider possibly sharing some concerns with God. He commands: CAST your anxiety on Him. Picture yourself literally throwing that stress off your shoulders and onto His. Why? Because He cares for you. Not just tolerates or endures you—actively cares.

God's shoulders are broad enough for your mortgage worries and your teenager's rebellion. His wisdom encompasses your work deadlines and your marriage struggles. When you try to carry it all yourself, you're robbing God of the opportunity to show Himself strong on your behalf.

Your kids need to see what you do with stress. Do you explode? Self-medicate? Withdraw? Or do they watch Dad take his burdens to God and find peace? Every time you choose prayer over panic, you're teaching them where to run when life gets heavy. God's power isn't just available for your stress—it's specifically designed for it. Let Him carry what's crushing you.

A PRAYER FOR YOU

Father, I'm drowning in stress and trying to hold it together. I cast every anxiety on You right now—the bills, the relationships, the fears. You care for me more than I can understand. Replace my stress with Your peace. Help my family see You carrying what I cannot. Amen.

YOUR CHALLENGE

Create a physical "stress cast" this week. Write your anxieties on paper, pray over them specifically, then throw the paper away or burn it safely. Make this casting visible—let your kids see you literally giving your stress to God. Explain what you're doing and why.

TAKE A MOMENT

Place your hand on your chest and feel your heartbeat. Take five deep breaths, and with each exhale, release one specific stress to God. Feel the physical relief of letting Him carry what was never yours to bear alone.

WEEK 16: SPEAKING FAITH INTO YOUR CHILDREN

GOD'S TRUTH

"Death and life are in the power of the tongue, and those who love it will eat its fruits."–Proverbs 18:21 (ESV)

DEVOTIONAL THOUGHT

Your words carry more weight than you realize. That off-hand comment about your son being "just like your lazy brother" or your daughter "never listening"—those words take root deep in their identity. But here's the flip side: your words also have the power to speak life, destiny, and faith into their souls.

When God wanted to change Abram's destiny, He changed his name to Abraham—father of nations. God spoke identity before it was reality. You have that same opportunity every day. Instead of "you never," try "I believe you can." Replace "why can't you" with "I see growth in you."

Speaking faith isn't about fake positivity or ignoring problems. It's about calling out the gold buried in the dirt. That struggling student? "God has given you a unique way of learning." That anxious child? "God is building courage in you." You're prophesying their future, not just describing their present.

Your children will face enough voices telling them what they can't do, who they'll never be, why they're not enough. Let

Dad's voice be different. Let it be the voice that speaks God's truth about their identity, potential, and worth. Years later, when life gets hard, they'll hear your words of faith echoing in their hearts, drowning out the lies.

A PRAYER FOR YOU

Lord, forgive me for careless words that have wounded instead of built up. Set a guard over my mouth. Help me speak faith, life, and destiny into my children. Show me what You see in them, and give me the words to call it forth. Let my voice echo Your love. Amen.

YOUR CHALLENGE

Each day this week, speak one specific faith statement to each child. Not generic praise, but targeted truth: "I see God developing leadership in you" or "Your kindness reflects Jesus." Watch their countenance change when Dad speaks faith instead of just correction.

TAKE A MOMENT

Think back to words spoken over you—positive or negative—that still echo in your mind. Consider the power those words have had in shaping you. Choose today to be intentional with the words you plant in your children's hearts.

WEEK 17: BEING A ROLE MODEL OF INTEGRITY

GOD'S TRUTH

"Whoever walks in integrity walks securely, but he who makes his ways crooked will be found out."–
Proverbs 10:9 (ESV)

DEVOTIONAL THOUGHT

Your kids are watching when you think they aren't. They see when you keep the extra change the cashier gave by mistake. They notice if your sick day is really a golf day. They hear you commit to something then bail when a better offer comes. These moments are teaching them whether integrity is real or just religious talk.

Integrity means being the same person in public and private. It's keeping your word even when it costs you. It's admitting mistakes instead of covering them. It's choosing the right thing even when no one would know. This isn't about perfection—it's about consistency between your values and your actions.

When you walk in integrity, you walk securely. No fear of being exposed, no elaborate lies to maintain, no anxiety about your kids discovering the "real" you. They already know the real you, and they see a man who, though imperfect, strives to live what he believes.

Your integrity or lack thereof will preach louder than any lesson you teach. When your kids see you return the wallet you found, tell the truth when it's uncomfortable, or keep commitments that have become inconvenient, they're learning that following God means something real. That security you walk in? It becomes the foundation they build their own lives upon.

A PRAYER FOR YOU

Father, reveal any areas where I'm not walking in integrity. Give me the courage to be the same man in private that I claim to be in public. Help me model honesty and consistency for my children, even when it's costly. Let them see authentic faith lived out. Amen.

YOUR CHALLENGE

This week, identify one area where you've been compromising—maybe it's your language when kids aren't around, your honesty about work hours, or commitments you've made. Take one concrete step toward integrity in that area. If appropriate, let your kids see you making the right choice.

TAKE A MOMENT

Consider the legacy you're leaving. When your children describe you to their children someday, will integrity be part of that description? Let that future testimony motivate present choices.

WEEK 18: FINDING GOD IN DRY SEASONS

GOD'S TRUTH

"As a deer pants for flowing streams, so pants my soul for you, O God."–Psalm 42:1 (ESV)

DEVOTIONAL THOUGHT

Sometimes your spiritual life feels like a desert. Prayers bounce off the ceiling. The Bible feels dry as dust. You go through the motions at church but feel nothing. Meanwhile, you're supposed to be leading your family spiritually. How do you give water when your own well is dry?

David knew this feeling. The man after God's own heart had seasons where his soul panted desperately for what seemed absent. Here's the truth that changes everything: dry seasons don't mean God has left. They mean He's teaching you to seek Him for who He is, not just what you feel.

Your kids need to see that faith isn't dependent on feelings. When they watch you persist in prayer during spiritual drought, they learn faithfulness. When you keep reading Scripture even when it feels empty, they understand commitment. When you worship without the emotional high, they discover that God is worthy regardless of your mood.

These desert seasons often precede breakthrough. The deep roots you're growing while searching for water will sustain you through future storms. Your children are learning that real faith survives when feelings fade. Keep seeking. The same God who led you to the desert will lead you through it. And your family is watching how faith works when it's hard.

A PRAYER FOR YOU

Lord, I'm so dry spiritually, but I choose to seek You anyway. Help me push through this desert season. Teach me to want You for who You are, not just what I feel. Let my kids see that faith persists even when emotions don't cooperate. Refresh my soul. Amen.

YOUR CHALLENGE

This week, maintain one spiritual discipline even though you don't feel like it—maybe reading one psalm each morning or praying for five minutes. Don't wait for feelings; just show up. Tell your family you're choosing faithfulness over feelings, modeling persistent faith for them.

TAKE A MOMENT

Remember a past season when God felt distant but later proved He was working behind the scenes. Trust that He's doing the same thing now, even in this dry place.

WEEK 19: THE POWER OF SMALL DAILY STEPS

GOD'S TRUTH

"And let us not grow weary of doing good, for in due season we will reap, if we do not give up."–Galatians 6:9 (ESV)

DEVOTIONAL THOUGHT

You want massive change overnight. The defiant child suddenly obedient, the broken marriage instantly healed, the financial pressure immediately relieved. But God often works through small, daily faithfulness. The kingdom of heaven is like a mustard seed—tiny beginnings, eventual transformation.

Every night you pray with your kids, you're planting seeds. Each time you choose patience over anger, you're watering growth. When you apologize for losing your temper, you're tending soil. These seem insignificant compared to the harvest you're hoping for, but don't grow weary. The compound effect of small, daily faithfulness is staggering.

Your children won't remember one grand gesture as much as thousands of small, consistent acts of love. The daily breakfast conversations matter more than the expensive vacation. The regular bedtime prayers outweigh the occasional spiritual event. Transformation happens through accumulation, not single moments.

That habit you're trying to build, that change you're attempting in your family culture—keep going. It feels like nothing's happening, but beneath the surface, roots are deepening. In due season, you'll see the fruit of today's faithfulness. Your kids are learning that lasting change comes through daily discipline, not dramatic moments. Don't give up. The small step you take today might be the one that changes everything.

A PRAYER FOR YOU

Father, I get discouraged when I don't see immediate results. Help me trust the power of small, daily faithfulness. Give me strength to keep planting, watering, and tending, even when I can't see growth. Remind me that You're working through my ordinary obedience. Amen.

YOUR CHALLENGE

Choose one small thing to do consistently this week—read one Bible verse at breakfast, give each child a specific encouragement before bed, or pray during your commute. Focus on consistency over complexity. Mark each day you do it, building momentum through small wins.

TAKE A MOMENT

Think about a positive habit or trait you have now that started with small, barely noticeable steps. Remember how those tiny beginnings led to real change. Apply that same patience to the changes you're pursuing in your family today.

WEEK 20: OVERCOMING THE PRESSURE TO BE PERFECT

GOD'S TRUTH

"But he said to me, 'My grace is sufficient for you, for my power is made perfect in weakness.'"–2 Corinthians 12:9 (ESV)

DEVOTIONAL THOUGHT

Social media shows you the highlight reels of perfect fathers. Church makes you feel like everyone else has it together. Your own father's voice echoes, telling you all the ways you're falling short. The pressure to be the perfect dad is crushing, and it's a lie that's stealing your joy and authenticity.

Here's freedom: God never asked you to be perfect. He asked you to be dependent. Your weaknesses aren't disqualifications—they're opportunities for His strength to shine. When your kids see you mess up and run to God for grace, they learn what to do with their own imperfections.

Perfectionism teaches your children that love must be earned through performance. But when they see you receiving God's grace for your failures, they understand that love is a gift, not a wage. Your mistakes, covered by grace, become powerful teaching moments about the gospel.

Stop exhausting yourself trying to be super-dad. Your children don't need a father who never fails; they need one who shows them what to do with failure. When you embrace your need for grace, you create a home where everyone can be human. God's power shows up best in weak, imperfect fathers who know they need Him. That's the kind of dad that raises kids who run to God, not from Him.

A PRAYER FOR YOU

Lord, I'm tired of pretending I have it all together. Thank You that Your grace is enough for my failures. Help me stop striving for perfection and start depending on Your strength. Let my kids see that grace is real and available for imperfect people like us. Amen.

YOUR CHALLENGE

This week, when you make a parenting mistake, resist the urge to hide it or minimize it. Instead, acknowledge it to your kids, ask forgiveness if needed, and share how God's grace covers you. Show them what depending on grace looks like in real time.

TAKE A MOMENT

Release yourself from one unrealistic expectation you've been carrying. Maybe it's being the fun dad, the coach dad, or the always-patient dad. Accept that you can be a good father without being perfect at everything.

WEEK 21: MANAGING ANGER WITH GRACE

GOD'S TRUTH

"Be angry and do not sin; do not let the sun go down on your anger."–Ephesians 4:26 (ESV)

DEVOTIONAL THOUGHT

The rage rises faster than you expect. Your teenager's disrespect, your toddler's defiance, your spouse's criticism—suddenly you're yelling words you'll regret, slamming doors, becoming the man you swore you'd never be. The look in your child's eyes shifts from defiance to fear, and shame floods your heart.

Paul acknowledges something crucial: anger itself isn't sin. It's what we do with it that matters. Jesus got angry at injustice and hypocrisy. The question isn't whether you'll feel anger as a father—you will. The question is whether you'll let it control you or whether you'll control it through God's grace.

Managing anger doesn't mean suppressing it until you explode. It means recognizing it, stepping back, and inviting God into that space. "Lord, I'm furious right now. Help me respond, not react." That pause between feeling and action is where grace lives.

Your children need to see that godly men get angry but don't sin in their anger. They need to watch you feel fury and choose patience, experience rage and select restraint. When you blow it—and you will—they need to see you own it, apologize, and try again. Every time you manage anger with grace, you're teaching them that emotions don't have to control us.

A PRAYER FOR YOU

Father, forgive me for the times anger has controlled me. Help me feel anger without sinning in it. Give me the self-control to pause before reacting. When I fail, give me humility to apologize. Teach my children through my example that grace is stronger than rage. Amen.

YOUR CHALLENGE

Identify your anger trigger this week—what consistently sets you off? Create a plan for that moment: step outside, count to ten, pray a specific prayer. Practice your pause. When you successfully manage anger even once, thank God for His grace that made it possible.

TAKE A MOMENT

Remember the last time you lost your temper with your family. Now imagine how that scene could have gone differently with a grace-filled pause. Commit that mental picture to memory for the next time anger rises.

WEEK 22: LEADING THROUGH LIFE'S STORMS

GOD'S TRUTH

"When you pass through the waters, I will be with you; and through the rivers, they shall not overwhelm you."–Isaiah 43:2 (ESV)

DEVOTIONAL THOUGHT

The diagnosis comes. The job disappears. The marriage shakes. Storms hit every family, and suddenly everyone's looking at Dad to see how we weather this. Your response in the storm teaches your children more about faith than a hundred sermons ever could.

Notice God doesn't promise to keep you from the waters— He promises to be with you in them. Your family doesn't need a father who pretends storms don't hurt. They need one who shows them where to anchor when everything's shaking. They're learning whether faith is just fair-weather or if it holds in the hurricane.

Leading through storms doesn't mean having all the answers. It means knowing Who does. When your kids see you drop to your knees instead of giving up, they learn where strength comes from. When they watch you worship through tears, they discover that God is worthy even in pain.

Your transparency in the storm matters. "Kids, Dad doesn't know how this will work out, but God does, and we're going to trust Him." That's not weakness—that's modeling dependent faith. The storms that threaten to destroy your family can become the very things that forge unshakeable faith. How you lead through this storm is writing a manual your children will reference in their own future tempests.

A PRAYER FOR YOU

Lord, this storm is overwhelming, but You promise to be with us in it. Help me lead my family with faith, not fear. Give me wisdom for decisions and strength to stand. Let my children see that You're trustworthy even when life is terrifying. Be our anchor. Amen.

YOUR CHALLENGE

Gather your family this week and honestly share (age-appropriately) about a storm you're facing together. Pray as a family, asking God for help. Let your children see that storms drive you toward God, not away from Him. Make faith in crisis a family experience.

TAKE A MOMENT

Recall a past storm that seemed insurmountable at the time. Remember how God brought you through. Let that testimony strengthen your faith for whatever storm you're facing now.

WEEK 23: THE STRENGTH OF SAYING "I'M SORRY"

GOD'S TRUTH

"Therefore, confess your sins to one another and pray for one another, that you may be healed."–
James 5:16 (ESV)

DEVOTIONAL THOUGHT

Three words that feel impossible: "I was wrong." Your pride screams that admitting fault undermines your authority. If you apologize, won't they respect you less? But here's the kingdom paradox: nothing builds your credibility like taking responsibility for your failures.

When you kneel down, look your child in the eye, and say, "Daddy was wrong. Will you forgive me?"—you're modeling the gospel. You're showing them that repentance isn't weakness; it's the pathway to healing. Every sincere apology teaches them that real men own their mistakes.

Your children already know you're imperfect—they live with you. What they're wondering is what you'll do about it. Will you blame, deflect, and justify? Or will you humble yourself and make it right? Your response to your own sin teaches them what to do with theirs.

That relationship with your teenager that feels broken? It might be waiting for your apology. The distance with your spouse your kids can feel? Maybe it starts healing with your confession. "I'm sorry" doesn't diminish your authority—it establishes it on the foundation of integrity. Your humility gives your family permission to be human too. When the leader admits weakness and seeks forgiveness, everyone else can drop their masks and find healing.

A PRAYER FOR YOU

Father, pride makes apologizing so hard. Give me the humility to admit when I'm wrong, especially to my family. Help me model repentance and reconciliation. Show me relationships that need the healing words "I'm sorry." Let my children see that strength includes taking responsibility. Amen.

YOUR CHALLENGE

This week, apologize for something specific to each family member—not a generic "sorry if I hurt you," but a specific ownership of wrong. Watch how sincere apology opens doors that seemed permanently closed. Notice how your vulnerability invites theirs.

TAKE A MOMENT

Think of someone who genuinely apologized to you and how it affected your relationship. Remember that feeling of respect and connection. Choose to give that same gift to your family through humble confession.

WEEK 24: RAISING KIDS WITH FAITH THAT LASTS

GOD'S TRUTH

"Train up a child in the way he should go; even when he is old he will not depart from it."–Proverbs 22:6 (ESV)

DEVOTIONAL THOUGHT

You can make them go to church, but you can't make them believe. This terrifying reality keeps Christian fathers awake at night. What if all the devotions, prayers, and Sunday schools don't stick? What if they walk away from faith the moment they leave your home?

Here's what matters more than perfect theology: authentic relationship. Your kids need to see that your faith isn't just rules and religion—it's a real relationship with a living God. When faith flows from relationship rather than regulation, it takes root deep in their hearts.

Faith that lasts is caught more than taught. They catch it when they see you reading your Bible because you want to, not because you should. They catch it when problems drive you to prayer instead of panic. They catch it when you serve others joyfully, forgive quickly, and worship genuinely.

Training them up doesn't mean forcing faith down their throats. It means creating an environment where faith can flourish naturally. Answer their hard questions honestly. Admit when you don't know something. Show them that doubt doesn't destroy faith—it often deepens it. The goal isn't raising kids who never question faith, but kids who know where to turn with their questions. Plant deep. Water consistently. Trust God with the harvest.

A PRAYER FOR YOU

Lord, I desperately want my children's faith to last beyond my home. Help me model authentic relationship with You, not just religious behavior. Give me wisdom to create an environment where faith grows naturally. I trust You to complete the work You've started in their hearts. Amen.

YOUR CHALLENGE

This week, share one story with your kids about how God has been real in your life—not a Bible story, but your story. Make it personal and honest, including doubts or struggles. Help them see that faith is about relationship, not just rules.

TAKE A MOMENT

Release the pressure of being responsible for your children's faith. You're called to plant and water, but only God can make it grow. Trust Him with the seeds you're faithfully sowing today.

WEEK 25: TRUSTING GOD WITH YOUR FINANCIAL DECISIONS

GOD'S TRUTH

"And my God will supply every need of yours according to his riches in glory in Christ Jesus."–
Philippians 4:19 (ESV)

DEVOTIONAL THOUGHT

The calculator doesn't lie. Bills exceed income. College tuition looms. Medical expenses pile up. You lie awake doing mental math that never adds up to enough. The weight of providing financially can crush your spirit and steal your peace. Your family feels the stress radiating from you.

Paul doesn't promise wealth—he promises provision for needs. There's freedom in that distinction. God knows exactly what your family needs, and His resources are unlimited. The same God who multiplied loaves and fishes is watching over your finances. He's not surprised by your bills or intimidated by your debt.

Your children are learning about money by watching you. Do they see Dad trusting God or consumed by worry? When money's tight, do they witness faith or fear? Your response to financial pressure is teaching them whether God is truly trustworthy or just theoretically good.

This doesn't mean being financially irresponsible. It means working diligently while trusting ultimately. It means teaching your kids that security comes from God, not bank accounts. When they see you tithing during tough times, praying over budgets, and choosing contentment over comparison, they're learning that God is Provider. Every financial crisis becomes an opportunity to show your family that God's faithfulness extends to every area—including the checkbook.

A PRAYER FOR YOU

Father, these financial pressures are crushing me. I choose to trust Your promise to supply our needs. Give me wisdom in financial decisions and faith when the math doesn't work. Help my family see that You're our true Provider. Replace my anxiety with peace. Amen.

YOUR CHALLENGE

This week, involve your family in praying over a specific financial need. Be honest (age-appropriately) about the challenge, then pray together, asking God to provide. When He answers—however He answers—celebrate His faithfulness together, teaching them that God cares about practical needs.

TAKE A MOMENT

Remember a time when God provided in an unexpected way. Let that testimony strengthen your faith for current financial challenges. He who has been faithful will be faithful again.

WEEK 26: FATHERHOOD IS YOUR GREATEST CALLING

GOD'S TRUTH

"Behold, children are a heritage from the Lord, the fruit of the womb a reward."–Psalm 127:3 (ESV)

DEVOTIONAL THOUGHT

The world measures success in promotions, portfolios, and platforms. But God measures differently. Those children interrupting your important work? They ARE your most important work. That calling you're searching for? You're living it every time you tuck them in, every time you choose their game over overtime, every time you speak truth into their hearts.

Fatherhood isn't something you do alongside your "real" calling—it IS your calling. God entrusted eternal souls to your care. No CEO position compares to shaping hearts for eternity. No achievement outweighs raising humans who love God and others well.

This calling won't make you famous. There's no salary for midnight comforting, no bonus for consistent presence, no promotion for patient instruction. But heaven's accounting is different. Every sacrifice, every prayer, every moment of guidance is recorded in a ledger that matters forever.

Your children are not interruptions to your purpose—they are your purpose. That business you're building? It's just a tool to serve your calling as their father. That ministry you lead? It means nothing if you lose your kids in the process. When you embrace fatherhood as your greatest calling, every ordinary moment becomes sacred. Diapers become discipleship. Carpooling becomes counseling. Bedtime becomes blessing. This is your masterwork, Dad. Everything else is just supporting cast.

A PRAYER FOR YOU

Lord, forgive me for seeing fatherhood as secondary to other callings. Help me embrace it as my greatest ministry. Give me eyes to see the eternal significance of raising these children. When I'm tempted to chase lesser things, remind me that these souls are my greatest work. Amen.

YOUR CHALLENGE

This week, when career demands compete with family time, consciously choose your children at least once. Skip the optional meeting for the school play. Leave work on time for dinner. Let your actions declare that fatherhood is your highest calling.

TAKE A MOMENT

Fast-forward to your final days. What will matter then—the deals closed or the children raised? Let that eternal perspective reshape how you view your calling as a father today.

WEEK 27: RECONNECTING WITH YOUR WIFE THROUGH FAITH

GOD'S TRUTH

"Therefore a man shall leave his father and his mother and hold fast to his wife, and they shall become one flesh."–Genesis 2:24 (ESV)

DEVOTIONAL THOUGHT

The kids consumed everything. Somewhere between diapers and driving lessons, you became co-managers of a household instead of lovers united in faith. You pass each other in the hallway, tag-team parenting duties, and fall into bed exhausted. Your children are watching two roommates, not one flesh.

Here's what your kids need to understand: Mom and Dad's marriage is the foundation of this family's security. When they see you pursuing their mother, they feel safe. When they witness you praying together, they understand covenant. When you choose date night over their activities sometimes, they learn that marriage requires intentional investment.

Reconnecting through faith means more than attending church together. It means praying for each other, not just the kids. It means studying God's Word as a couple, letting Him speak into your marriage. It means forgiving quickly because grace covers you both.

Your marriage is the first gospel your children will read. When they see you serving your wife sacrificially, they understand Christ's love for the church. When they watch you reconcile after arguments, they learn that love perseveres. Your thriving marriage becomes their template for future relationships. Investing in your marriage isn't taking away from your kids—it's giving them the security of parents who are truly one.

A PRAYER FOR YOU

Lord, help me prioritize my marriage in the chaos of parenting. Rekindle the spiritual connection with my wife. Help us pursue You together, not just manage life together. Let our children see a marriage that reflects Your love. Give us time, energy, and desire to reconnect. Amen.

YOUR CHALLENGE

This week, initiate one spiritual activity with your wife—pray together before bed, share what God's teaching you, or simply ask how you can pray for her. Make your marriage's spiritual health as important as your parenting. Show your kids that Mom and Dad pursue God together.

TAKE A MOMENT

Remember when you first fell in love with your wife. Thank God for her, specifically for three qualities that make her a great mother. Let gratitude reignite affection that may have been buried under responsibility.

WEEK 28: GROWING STRONGER IN GOD'S WORD

GOD'S TRUTH

"All Scripture is breathed out by God and profitable for teaching, for reproof, for correction, and for training in righteousness."–2 Timothy 3:16 (ESV)

DEVOTIONAL THOUGHT

Your Bible sits on the nightstand, gathering dust and guilt. You know you should read it more, but where's the time? Between work demands and family needs, diving into Scripture feels like another task on an impossible list. Yet you know your spiritual strength depends on it.

Here's the shift: God's Word isn't another obligation—it's your lifeline. Every page contains wisdom for the situation you're facing today. That teenage rebellion? There's guidance for that. The financial stress? God addresses it. The marriage tension? Scripture speaks to it. This isn't ancient history; it's living truth for modern fathers.

Your kids notice whether Dad's Bible is decorative or deployed. When they see you mining Scripture for wisdom, they learn where answers come from. When problems arise and you say, "Let's see what God says about this," you're teaching them that the Bible is practical, not just spiritual.

Start small if you must. One verse during coffee. One psalm before bed. One proverb during lunch. God's Word is like compound interest—small, consistent deposits yield tremendous returns. As you grow stronger in Scripture, your family benefits from the overflow. You can't give what you don't have, and what your family needs most is a father anchored in God's truth.

A PRAYER FOR YOU

Father, forgive me for neglecting Your Word. Help me hunger for Scripture like food. Give me discipline to read consistently and wisdom to apply what I learn. Let Your Word strengthen me to lead my family well. Make the Bible come alive to me again. Amen.

YOUR CHALLENGE

This week, read one chapter of Proverbs each day—there are 31, one for each day of the month. Share one practical insight from your reading with your family at dinner. Show them that God's Word speaks to real life, and Dad is learning too.

TAKE A MOMENT

Open your Bible right now to Psalm 23. Read it slowly, imagining God speaking directly to you about your current struggles. Let His Word minister to your father's heart before you minister to others.

WEEK 29: RAISING KIDS WHO REFLECT GOD'S LOVE

GOD'S TRUTH

"A new commandment I give to you, that you love one another: just as I have loved you, you also are to love one another."–John 13:34 (ESV)

DEVOTIONAL THOUGHT

You can teach your kids to be successful, athletic, and smart. But if they don't know how to love, you've missed the mark. The world desperately needs humans who reflect God's love—and that training starts at your dinner table.

Love isn't just being nice when life's easy. It's choosing kindness when someone's annoying. It's sharing when you'd rather keep. It's forgiving when you've been hurt. Your children learn this not from lectures but from watching you. How you treat the difficult waiter, the slow cashier, the neighbor with different politics—you're teaching love or its absence.

When your kids see you serving others without recognition, they learn love isn't transactional. When they watch you forgive their mother quickly, they understand grace. When you show patience with their mistakes, they experience God's patient love through you.

Raising kids who reflect God's love means creating opportunities to practice it. Serve together at the food bank. Take meals to sick neighbors. Include the lonely kid. These aren't just nice activities—they're love laboratories where your children learn to see others through God's eyes. The world will know your children are Christians not by their church attendance or Bible knowledge, but by their love. That love is caught in your home before it's released to the world.

A PRAYER FOR YOU

Lord, help me model Your love so clearly that my children can't help but reflect it. Teach me to love the unlovable, serve without recognition, and forgive quickly. Let our home be a training ground for the kind of love that changes the world. Fill us with Your love. Amen.

YOUR CHALLENGE

This week, do one act of radical love as a family—serve someone who can't repay you, forgive someone who hurt you, or include someone typically excluded. Discuss afterward how it felt to love like Jesus loves. Make love practical, not theoretical.

TAKE A MOMENT

Think about someone who showed you God's love when you didn't deserve it. Consider how that impacted you. Commit to being that person for someone else, with your children watching and learning.

WEEK 30: GOD'S GRACE FOR YOUR PARENTING MISTAKES

GOD'S TRUTH

"If we confess our sins, he is faithful and just to forgive us our sins and to cleanse us from all unrighteousness."–1 John 1:9 (ESV)

DEVOTIONAL THOUGHT

The parenting fails haunt you at night. The time you yelled too harshly. The promise you broke. The important moment you missed because work seemed more urgent. The enemy whispers that you've ruined them, that the damage is irreversible. But God's grace speaks louder than your guilt.

Every father fails. Abraham lied about his wife. David was absent. Even the patriarch Jacob played favorites. Yet God used these imperfect fathers in His perfect plan. Your mistakes don't disqualify you—they qualify you for grace.

Your children don't need a father who never fails; they need one who shows them what to do with failure. When you confess your parenting sins to God and receive His forgiveness, you're modeling the gospel. When you make amends with your children, you're teaching them that relationships can be restored.

Grace doesn't erase consequences, but it does enable fresh starts. That harsh word can't be unsaid, but it can be redeemed through humble apology. That missed moment is gone, but future presence can heal past absence. God's grace is bigger than your biggest parenting mistake. Stop rehearsing your failures and start receiving His forgiveness. Your kids need to see that grace is real, available, and powerful enough to cover even Dad's mistakes.

A PRAYER FOR YOU

Father, I've failed my kids in so many ways. Thank You that Your grace covers all my parenting mistakes. Help me receive Your forgiveness and extend it to myself. Show me how to make things right where I can, and trust You to redeem what I can't fix. Amen.

YOUR CHALLENGE

This week, release yourself from one parenting mistake you've been carrying. Confess it to God, receive His forgiveness, and if appropriate, make amends with your child. Then let it go. Show your family that grace is real and available for all of us.

TAKE A MOMENT

Write down your biggest parenting regret on a piece of paper. Pray over it, asking God's forgiveness. Then destroy the paper as a physical reminder that God has removed that sin as far as east is from west.

WEEK 31: THE POWER OF PRAYER IN FATHERHOOD

GOD'S TRUTH

"The prayer of a righteous person has great power as it is working."–James 5:16b (ESV)

DEVOTIONAL THOUGHT

You feel powerless watching your child struggle. The anxiety that grips your teenager. The friend drama crushing your daughter. The temptations surrounding your son. You can't fight every battle for them, but you can fight every battle on your knees.

Prayer isn't your last resort when everything else fails—it's your first line of defense. Every prayer you pray over your children is actively working, even when you can't see results. Those morning prayers over breakfast, the silent petitions during their games, the midnight intercessions when they're out with friends—all of it has power.

Your children may not always listen to your advice, but God always hears your prayers. You're appealing to the One who can change hearts, arrange circumstances, and protect in ways you never could. When you pray Scripture over your kids, you're aligning your requests with God's will, and that's unstoppable power.

Prayer changes things, but it also changes you. As you pray for patience with your strong-willed child, God transforms your heart. As you intercede for their future spouse, you gain eternal perspective. As you battle for them spiritually, you become the warrior father they need. Your prayers are shaping their destiny more than you realize. Keep praying, Dad. Heaven is listening, and hell is trembling.

A PRAYER FOR YOU

Lord, increase my faith in the power of prayer. Help me cover my children consistently in prayer, not just in crisis. Give me specific ways to pray for each child. Let them know that Dad talks to God about them constantly. Make me a warrior on my knees. Amen.

YOUR CHALLENGE

Create a prayer rhythm this week—pray for one specific thing for each child every day. Maybe protection on Monday, wisdom on Tuesday, friendships on Wednesday. Write it down if needed. Let your kids know you're praying specifically for them and ask how you can pray better.

TAKE A MOMENT

Consider the most impossible situation one of your children faces right now. Spend the next five minutes praying boldly for breakthrough, remembering that your prayers have great power as they're working.

WEEK 32: TEACHING RESILIENCE THROUGH FAITH

GOD'S TRUTH

"Not only that, but we rejoice in our sufferings, knowing that suffering produces endurance, and endurance produces character, and character produces hope."–Romans 5:3-4 (ESV)

DEVOTIONAL THOUGHT

Your instinct is to shield them from every disappointment. The team that cuts them. The friend who betrays them. The dream that crumbles. But what if your children need some struggles to develop the strength they'll need for life?

Resilience isn't built in comfort—it's forged in challenges. When you rush to fix every problem, you rob your children of the chance to develop endurance. When you fight all their battles, they never learn to stand. Faith-based resilience means teaching them that God uses every struggle for growth.

This doesn't mean being harsh or unsupportive. It means walking alongside them through difficulties instead of removing every obstacle. It means praying with them through problems instead of just solving them. It means helping them see God's purposes in their pain.

When your child faces disappointment, help them find God in it. What is He teaching? How is He growing them? What strength is being developed? When they learn to ask these questions, they stop being victims of circumstances and become students of sovereignty. Every trial becomes a training ground for greater things. The resilience you're building today through faith will sustain them through storms you won't be there to weather with them.

A PRAYER FOR YOU

Father, give me wisdom to know when to protect and when to let them struggle. Help me teach my children to find You in their difficulties. Build resilience in them that's rooted in faith, not just determination. Use their trials to produce endurance, character, and hope. Amen.

YOUR CHALLENGE

This week, when your child faces a difficulty, resist the urge to immediately fix it. Instead, sit with them, pray with them, and help them see what God might be developing through this challenge. Guide them to find their own God-directed solution.

TAKE A MOMENT

Remember a struggle from your past that built strength you still use today. Thank God for that difficult season and consider sharing that story with your children, helping them see purpose in their own challenges.

WEEK 33: FINDING REST IN GOD'S PRESENCE

GOD'S TRUTH

"Come to me, all who labor and are heavy laden, and I will give you rest."–Matthew 11:28 (ESV)

DEVOTIONAL THOUGHT

Exhaustion is your constant companion. Physical tiredness from long days. Emotional drainage from teenage drama. Mental fatigue from endless decisions. Spiritual depletion from pouring out more than you're taking in. You're running on empty, and your family gets the fumes.

Jesus doesn't offer a vacation or a day off—He offers Himself. Rest isn't found in the absence of responsibility but in the presence of God. When you come to Him with your weariness, He doesn't shame you for being tired. He invites you to lay down the burdens you were never meant to carry alone.

Your children need to see that Dad knows where to find rest. Not in entertainment or escape, but in God's presence. When they watch you retreating to pray instead of imploding from stress, they learn where renewal comes from. When you choose worship over worry, they see that peace is possible.

Rest isn't laziness—it's wisdom. Even God rested on the seventh day, not from exhaustion but as an example. When you model rhythms of rest and renewal in God's presence, you're teaching your family that burning out isn't noble. Regular rest in God's presence isn't selfish; it's essential. You can't pour from an empty cup, and your family needs you filled.

A PRAYER FOR YOU

Lord, I'm so tired. Thank You for inviting me to find rest in You. Help me stop wearing exhaustion like a badge of honor. Teach me to regularly retreat to Your presence for renewal. Show my family that true rest comes from You, not just sleep. Restore my soul. Amen.

YOUR CHALLENGE

This week, schedule fifteen minutes daily to simply sit in God's presence—not requesting, not reading, just resting. Put it on your calendar like an appointment. Let your family see you protecting this time, teaching them that rest in God is priority, not luxury.

TAKE A MOMENT

Right now, take five deep breaths. With each exhale, release a burden to God. With each inhale, receive His rest. Feel His presence bringing peace to your weary soul.

WEEK 34: BREAKING FREE FROM GENERATIONAL STRUGGLES

GOD'S TRUTH

"Therefore, if anyone is in Christ, he is a new creation. The old has passed away; behold, the new has come."–2 Corinthians 5:17 (ESV)

DEVOTIONAL THOUGHT

You catch yourself mid-sentence and freeze. You sound exactly like your father—and not in a good way. The anger, the distance, the criticism you swore you'd never repeat is flowing from your mouth to your child's ears. Generational patterns have a way of surviving despite our best intentions.

But here's the gospel truth: you're a new creation in Christ. The chains that bound your father don't have to bind you. The struggles that plagued previous generations can stop with you. God's power is greater than your family's patterns.

Breaking generational struggles requires honest recognition. What unhealthy patterns did you inherit? Rage? Addiction? Emotional absence? Workaholism? Name them, claim Christ's power over them, and choose differently. It's not easy, but it's possible.

Your children are watching you rewrite the family story. When you choose vulnerability over emotional walls, you're breaking chains. When you stay present instead of escaping, you're creating new patterns. When you apologize instead of defending, you're charting a new course. You might be the transitional generation—the one who inherited pain but passes on healing. The struggles stop here. Your children and their children will thank you for the battles you're fighting today in private.

A PRAYER FOR YOU

Father, reveal the generational patterns I need to break. Give me courage to face family struggles honestly. Through Your power, help me be the one who stops destructive cycles. Let my children inherit blessing, not bondage. Make me truly new in Christ, free from old patterns. Amen.

YOUR CHALLENGE

Identify one specific generational pattern you want to break. Share it with your spouse or a trusted friend for accountability. Take one concrete step this week to choose differently than previous generations did. Let your kids see you creating new, healthier patterns.

TAKE A MOMENT

Think about the legacy you want to leave versus the one you inherited. Thank God that in Christ, you have the power to change your family tree. You're not doomed to repeat the past.

WEEK 35: HELPING YOUR KIDS DISCOVER THEIR CALLING

GOD'S TRUTH

"For we are his workmanship, created in Christ Jesus for good works, which God prepared beforehand, that we should walk in them."–
Ephesians 2:10 (ESV)

DEVOTIONAL THOUGHT

You watch your child and wonder: What will they become? The pressure to guide them toward the right career, college, or path feels overwhelming. But what if their calling is less about what they'll do and more about who they'll become in Christ?

God created each of your children with intentionality. That child who questions everything might be designed for apologetics. The one who organizes their siblings could be a future leader. The quiet one who notices others' pain might be called to counseling. Your job isn't to decide their calling— it's to help them discover how God wired them.

This means paying attention to their natural gifts, not just pushing your preferences. It means celebrating the athlete and the artist equally. It means asking, "What makes you come alive?" instead of "What will make you successful?" It means teaching them that calling is about serving God and others, not just earning income.

When you help your children see themselves as God's workmanship with prepared purposes, everything shifts. School becomes preparation, not just obligation. Struggles become training, not just trials. Their unique personality becomes purposeful design, not random chance. You're raising world-changers, Dad. Help them discover the specific way God designed them to change it.

A PRAYER FOR YOU

Lord, help me see each child's unique design and calling. Give me wisdom to nurture their gifts without imposing my dreams. Show me how to guide without controlling, encourage without pressuring. Help them discover the good works You've prepared specifically for them. Amen.

YOUR CHALLENGE

This week, have a one-on-one conversation with each child about what makes them come alive. Listen without directing. Ask what they think God might be preparing them for. Affirm the gifts you see in them that they might not recognize in themselves.

TAKE A MOMENT

Consider each of your children's unique gifts and passions. Thank God for the specific way He's designed each one. Ask Him to show you how to better nurture their individual callings.

WEEK 36: CREATING A HOME THAT FEELS SAFE

GOD'S TRUTH

"By wisdom a house is built, and by understanding it is established; by knowledge the rooms are filled with all precious and pleasant riches."–Proverbs 24:3-4 (ESV)

DEVOTIONAL THOUGHT

Your home's atmosphere matters more than its appearance. You can have granite countertops and designer furniture, but if your kids walk on eggshells, you've failed. A safe home isn't about locks on doors—it's about peace in hearts.

Safety means your children know they can fail without losing your love. They can share struggles without facing explosion. They can be themselves without performing for acceptance. This kind of safety doesn't happen accidentally—it's built through wisdom, established through understanding, and filled by knowledge of what truly matters.

When voices stay calm during conflict, safety grows. When mistakes trigger teaching instead of tirades, trust builds. When Dad admits his own struggles, walls come down. Your home becomes a refuge from the world's harsh judgments, a place where grace lives and love never leaves.

This doesn't mean no boundaries or consequences. True safety includes structure and discipline. But it means those boundaries exist within unshakeable love. Your children should fear disappointing you but never fear losing you. In a world that feels increasingly unsafe, your home can be an embassy of heaven—a place where Kingdom values rule and perfect love casts out fear.

A PRAYER FOR YOU

Father, help me create a home that feels safe for my family. Remove any fear I've introduced through anger or unpredictability. Fill our home with Your peace. Let each family member feel valued, heard, and unconditionally loved within these walls. Make our home a refuge. Amen.

YOUR CHALLENGE

Ask each family member this week: "What would make our home feel safer for you?" Listen without defending. Take one practical step toward creating the safety they need—maybe it's controlling your temper, being more predictable, or simply listening better.

TAKE A MOMENT

Walk through your home and pray over each space. Ask God to fill every room with His peace and safety. Commit to being the guardian of your home's atmosphere, not just its physical security.

WEEK 37: EMBRACING EVERY SEASON OF FATHERHOOD

GOD'S TRUTH

"For everything there is a season, and a time for every matter under heaven."–Ecclesiastes 3:1 (ESV)

DEVOTIONAL THOUGHT

You miss the baby cuddles but dread the teenage years. You long for the simplicity of young children but feel overwhelmed by their constant needs. Every season of fatherhood brings unique joys and distinct challenges, and you're always tempted to wish for a different one.

But God has you in this exact season for a reason. The exhausting toddler years are building your patience. The questioning preteen phase is deepening your wisdom. The letting-go teenage years are teaching you trust. Each season is preparing you and them for what's next.

Embracing the current season means being fully present in it. Stop wishing for easier days or dreading harder ones. The child in front of you today will never be this age again. Tomorrow they'll be one day older, one step further from childhood, one moment closer to independence.

Every season is sacred. Diapers are as holy as diplomas when done for God's glory. Teaching them to tie shoes matters as much as teaching them to drive. Each phase of fatherhood is a gift, even the hard ones. When you embrace rather than endure the season you're in, you find grace specifically designed for these exact challenges. God's mercies aren't just new every morning—they're perfectly timed for every season.

A PRAYER FOR YOU

Lord, help me embrace this exact season of fatherhood. Forgive me for wishing it away or dreading what's coming. Give me eyes to see the gifts hidden in today's challenges. Help me be fully present in this phase, knowing it won't last forever. Thank You for season-specific grace. Amen.

YOUR CHALLENGE

This week, identify one thing you love about your current season of fatherhood and one thing you find challenging. Thank God for both, asking Him to show you what He's teaching you through this exact phase. Share with your kids something you appreciate about their current age.

TAKE A MOMENT

Look at an old photo of your children. Remember that season—its challenges and joys. Now appreciate how far you've all come and trust God with the seasons still ahead.

WEEK 38: CONQUERING FEAR ABOUT THE FUTURE

GOD'S TRUTH

"Fear not, for I am with you; be not dismayed, for I am your God; I will strengthen you, I will help you, I will uphold you with my righteous right hand."–
Isaiah 41:10 (ESV)

DEVOTIONAL THOUGHT

Fear whispers constantly. What if they rebel? What if they get hurt? What if the economy crashes? What if you're not enough? The "what ifs" of fatherhood can paralyze you, stealing today's joy with tomorrow's imagined tragedies.

But God speaks louder than fear: "I am with you." Not "I might be" or "I'll try to be"—I AM. The same God who's brought you this far won't abandon you now. Every future scenario that terrifies you, He's already walked through. He's not worried about your family's tomorrow.

Your children are learning how to face the future by watching you. When they see Dad consumed by anxiety, they learn fear. But when they watch you taking concerns to God and finding peace, they discover that faith is stronger than fear.

This doesn't mean ignoring real concerns or failing to prepare. It means recognizing that your family's future isn't in your hands alone—it's held by the One who upholds all things. Every fear about tomorrow is an opportunity to trust

God today. Your kids need a father who faces the future with faith, not fear. When you conquer anxiety through God's promises, you're teaching them that tomorrow isn't scary when you know Who holds it.

A PRAYER FOR YOU

Father, fear about my family's future is stealing my peace. I choose to trust that You're already in tomorrow. Strengthen my faith when anxiety rises. Help my children see that we don't have to fear the future because You're already there. Replace my fear with faith. Amen.

YOUR CHALLENGE

Write down your three biggest fears about your family's future. Next to each fear, write a promise from Scripture that addresses it. When anxiety rises this week, speak those promises out loud. Let your kids hear you choosing faith over fear.

TAKE A MOMENT

Take a deep breath and release every "what if" to God. Trust that the One who holds the universe together can handle your family's future. Rest in His sovereignty over tomorrow.

WEEK 39: FINDING JOY IN THE LITTLE THINGS

GOD'S TRUTH

"This is the day that the Lord has made; let us rejoice and be glad in it."–Psalm 118:24 (ESV)

DEVOTIONAL THOUGHT

You're waiting for the big moments to bring joy. The promotion, the vacation, the graduation. Meanwhile, you're missing the daily gifts scattered like breadcrumbs through your ordinary life. Your child's laugh at a silly joke. The way they still want to hold your hand. Their excitement when you walk through the door.

Joy isn't found in perfect circumstances—it's discovered in present awareness. Today, this ordinary Tuesday, is a day the Lord made specifically for you and your family. There's something to rejoice about hidden in its mundane moments if you'll just look.

The little things are actually the big things wearing disguise. That bedtime prayer you're tired of repeating? It's shaping eternity. The family dinner you almost skipped? It's building bonds that last lifetimes. The walk around the block? It might be when your teenager finally opens up.

Your children don't need expensive experiences to feel joy—they need a dad who finds delight in daily life with them. When you celebrate small victories, laugh at simple pleasures, and find God in ordinary moments, you're teaching them that joy isn't circumstantial. Every day holds treasures if you have eyes to see them. Stop waiting for joy to arrive and start recognizing it's already here.

A PRAYER FOR YOU

Lord, open my eyes to the joy hiding in ordinary moments. Help me stop waiting for perfect circumstances to be grateful. Teach me to rejoice in this day You've made, with all its imperfections. Let my children see that joy is found in Your presence, not perfect situations. Amen.

YOUR CHALLENGE

Each day this week, identify and celebrate one small joy with your family—the first flower of spring, a good grade on a quiz, everyone being healthy today. Make finding joy a family practice. Watch how this shifts your home's atmosphere from surviving to thriving.

TAKE A MOMENT

Right now, list five small things about your life as a dad that bring you joy. Let gratitude for these simple gifts flood your heart. Thank God for the little things that are really the big things.

WEEK 40: LOVING YOUR FAMILY THROUGH HARD TIMES

GOD'S TRUTH

"Love bears all things, believes all things, hopes all things, endures all things."–1 Corinthians 13:7 (ESV)

DEVOTIONAL THOUGHT

Hard times test everything. The diagnosis that changes everything. The job loss that threatens stability. The rebellious child who breaks your heart. When life gets brutal, love gets real. It's easy to love when everyone's happy and healthy. But hard times reveal whether your love has deep roots or shallow sentiment.

Love that bears all things doesn't mean pretending everything's fine. It means carrying the weight together. When your teenager makes destructive choices, love believes God's not finished with them. When your marriage feels broken, love hopes for restoration. When chronic illness exhausts everyone, love endures without keeping score.

Your family is watching how Dad loves when life hurts. Do you withdraw into yourself or draw the family closer? Do you become bitter or better? Your love during trials becomes their reference point for God's unfailing love. They learn that real love doesn't depend on good circumstances.

Hard times can fracture families or forge them stronger. The difference is love that refuses to quit. When you choose patience over frustration, presence over escape, and hope over despair, you're teaching your family that love is stronger than any storm. Your love becomes the shelter where they weather life's worst moments.

A PRAYER FOR YOU

Father, loving my family through this hard season feels impossible some days. Fill me with Your love that bears, believes, hopes, and endures all things. Help me be the steady presence they need when everything else feels shaky. Let Your love flow through me when mine runs dry. Amen.

YOUR CHALLENGE

This week, identify who in your family is struggling most right now. Show them extra love in their specific love language—maybe that's quality time, words of affirmation, or acts of service. Let them know that Dad's love doesn't waver when times get tough.

TAKE A MOMENT

Remember a time someone loved you through a difficult season. Feel the impact of that steadfast love. Now commit to being that same anchor of love for your family in whatever storm you're facing.

WEEK 41: BECOMING A DAD WHO TRULY LISTENS

GOD'S TRUTH

"Know this, my beloved brothers: let every person be quick to hear, slow to speak, slow to anger."–
James 1:19 (ESV)

DEVOTIONAL THOUGHT

You're great at giving advice, solving problems, and sharing wisdom. But when did you last truly listen? Not waiting for your turn to talk, not formulating your response, but genuinely hearing your child's heart? Your family doesn't always need Dad the fixer—sometimes they just need Dad the listener.

Being quick to hear means putting down your phone, making eye contact, and entering their world. It means listening to the emotion behind the words. Your teenager's anger might be hiding hurt. Your young child's endless chatter contains clues to their inner world. Your wife's complaints might be requests for connection.

Listening is love in action. When you truly hear your children, they feel valued. When you listen without immediately judging or correcting, they learn to trust you with deeper things. The child who knows Dad will listen about small stuff will come to Dad with big stuff later.

God gave you two ears and one mouth for a reason. Your children don't need another lecturer—the world's full of those. They need someone who cares enough to understand before being understood. When you become a dad who truly listens, you become a safe place where hearts can be honest. That's where real relationship happens.

A PRAYER FOR YOU

Lord, forgive me for being too quick to speak and too slow to listen. Help me hear what my family is really saying, not just their words but their hearts. Give me patience to listen fully before responding. Make me a safe place where my family feels heard and understood. Amen.

YOUR CHALLENGE

This week, when a family member comes to talk, practice the "three-minute rule"—listen for three full minutes without interrupting, advising, or correcting. Just listen. Ask questions to understand better. Watch how this changes the depth of your conversations.

TAKE A MOMENT

Think about the last time someone really listened to you—how it felt to be truly heard. Resolve to give that gift to your family today. Put away distractions and be fully present for the next conversation.

WEEK 42: TRUSTING GOD TO COMPLETE THE PICTURE

GOD'S TRUTH

"And I am sure of this, that he who began a good work in you will bring it to completion at the day of Jesus Christ."–Philippians 1:6 (ESV)

DEVOTIONAL THOUGHT

You look at your children and see unfinished work. The character flaws that persist. The faith that wavers. The potential that's unrealized. Some days you wonder if all your prayers, teaching, and effort are making any difference. The picture looks nothing like what you'd hoped.

But you're seeing an incomplete painting. God's not finished yet. That strong-willed child who exhausts you? God's developing a leader. The sensitive one who seems fragile? God's crafting a heart of compassion. The rebellious teenager pushing boundaries? God might be forging an independent thinker who'll change the world.

Your job isn't to complete the picture—it's to trust the Artist. Every prayer you pray is a brushstroke. Every truth you teach adds color. Every moment of love adds depth. You can't see the masterpiece yet because it's still being painted.

This requires patience that only comes from faith. When progress seems slow or backwards, remember God's timeline isn't yours. He's working on an eternal canvas, not a temporary sketch. What looks like disaster might be preparation for destiny. Trust Him to complete what He started. Your children's stories aren't over. The God who began good work in them is faithful to finish it.

A PRAYER FOR YOU

Father, I get impatient wanting to see the finished product in my children. Help me trust Your process and timeline. When I can't see progress, remind me You're still working. Give me faith to believe You'll complete the beautiful work You've started in each of them. Amen.

YOUR CHALLENGE

Choose the child you're most concerned about right now. This week, instead of focusing on what's wrong, look for evidence of God's ongoing work—small improvements, character growth, or lessons being learned. Thank God for the work in progress, trusting Him with the outcome.

TAKE A MOMENT

Picture each of your children as adults, complete in Christ. Thank God in advance for the finished work He's creating. Let this eternal perspective encourage you through today's incomplete picture.

WEEK 43: LEADING WITH HUMILITY AND STRENGTH

GOD'S TRUTH

"But he gives more grace. Therefore it says, 'God opposes the proud but gives grace to the humble.'"–
James 4:6 (ESV)

DEVOTIONAL THOUGHT

The world tells you leadership means never showing weakness, never admitting uncertainty, never backing down. But God's kingdom operates differently. True strength is humble enough to admit need. Real leadership acknowledges limitations. The strongest fathers are those who know they need God's grace.

Humility doesn't mean being a doormat. It means leading from a position of dependence on God rather than confidence in yourself. When your children see you seeking God's wisdom for decisions, they learn dependence. When you admit you don't have all the answers, they learn it's okay to need help.

Pride says, "I've got this." Humility says, "God, I need You for this." Pride defends every decision. Humility can admit mistakes. Pride needs to be right. Humility needs to be righteous. Your children don't need a father who's never wrong—they need one who handles being wrong with grace.

When you lead with humility, God promises more grace. That grace flows through you to your family. They feel the difference between a father forcing his will and one following God's will. Humble strength creates an atmosphere where everyone can grow, fail, and try again. It's the perfect blend—strong enough to lead, humble enough to be led.

A PRAYER FOR YOU

Lord, pride comes so naturally, but I need Your grace more than my ego. Help me lead with humble strength, admitting when I'm wrong and seeking Your wisdom always. Show my children that true strength comes from dependence on You, not confidence in myself. Amen.

YOUR CHALLENGE

This week, involve your family in a decision you'd normally make alone. Admit you need wisdom and pray together about it. Let them see that Dad seeks input and God's guidance rather than ruling by decree. Model humble leadership that invites participation.

TAKE A MOMENT

Consider an area where pride has been driving your leadership. Confess it to God and ask for the humility to lead differently. Remember that God gives grace to the humble—grace your family desperately needs.

WEEK 44: FINDING PURPOSE IN SACRIFICES

GOD'S TRUTH

"Greater love has no one than this, that someone lay down his life for his friends."—John 15:13 (ESV)

DEVOTIONAL THOUGHT

You've given up so much. The career advancement you passed up for family time. The hobbies abandoned for kids' activities. The dreams deferred for doctor bills and school supplies. Some days the sacrifices feel like losses, and resentment creeps in.

But what if every sacrifice is actually an investment? That promotion you declined to coach little league? You were building relationship. The golf game you skipped for the school play? You were communicating value. The new truck you didn't buy to afford braces? You were choosing their future over your comfort.

Jesus redefined sacrifice as love in action. Every time you lay down your life—your time, desires, resources—for your family, you're demonstrating the gospel. Your children are learning that love costs something and they're worth the price.

The world measures success by what you accumulate. God measures it by what you're willing to sacrifice for others. Those sacrifices that feel like losses are actually the building blocks of legacy. Years from now, your children won't remember what you gave up, but they'll never forget that you chose them. Every sacrifice whispers to their hearts: "You matter more than anything I could have had instead."

A PRAYER FOR YOU

Father, help me see purpose in the sacrifices fatherhood requires. When I'm tempted toward resentment, remind me that every sacrifice is an act of love. Show me that what I'm giving up is nothing compared to what I'm building. Give me joy in laying down my life for my family. Amen.

YOUR CHALLENGE

This week, make one willing sacrifice for each family member—give up something you want to do for something they need. Do it joyfully, without mentioning the sacrifice. Let them experience being chosen over other options. Notice how sacrifice becomes worship when done with the right heart.

TAKE A MOMENT

List three things you've sacrificed for your family. Now re-imagine them not as losses but as investments in eternal relationships. Thank God for the privilege of having someone worth sacrificing for.

WEEK 45: REKINDLING YOUR PASSION FOR FATHERHOOD

GOD'S TRUTH

"Never be lacking in zeal, but keep your spiritual fervor, serving the Lord."–Romans 12:11 (ESV)

DEVOTIONAL THOUGHT

Somewhere between the sleepless infant nights and the stressful teenage years, the passion dimmed. Fatherhood became duty instead of delight. You still love your kids, but the joy has been buried under responsibility. You're going through the motions, and everyone feels it.

Passion isn't about feeling excited all the time—it's about remembering why this matters. Your role as father is literally shaping eternal souls. You're not just raising kids; you're raising future world-changers, Kingdom-builders, and image-bearers of God. If that doesn't stir something in you, you've forgotten the magnitude of your calling.

Rekindling passion starts with returning to the source. When your spiritual fervor for God grows cold, everything else follows. But when you're alive in Christ, that life overflows into every role, including fatherhood. Your kids need to see that being their dad brings you joy, not just exhaustion.

This might mean changing perspective, dropping unnecessary burdens, or simply remembering to play again. When did you last laugh with them instead of just managing them?

When did you last marvel at the privilege of being called "Dad"? The passion is still there, perhaps buried under fatigue and frustration. Let God breathe fresh wind on those cooling embers.

A PRAYER FOR YOU

Lord, I've let duty replace delight in fatherhood. Rekindle my passion for this calling. Help me see my children through fresh eyes and remember what a privilege it is to be their dad. Restore my spiritual fervor so it overflows into joyful fatherhood. Make me excited about this role again. Amen.

YOUR CHALLENGE

This week, do something with your kids that you used to love but haven't done lately—throw a football, build with Legos, have a dance party. Forget your age and responsibilities for an hour. Let yourself enjoy being Dad again. Watch how play rekindles passion.

TAKE A MOMENT

Remember the moment you first became a father—the overwhelming joy and sense of purpose. That same child who made you a dad still needs you. Let that original wonder reignite your passion for fatherhood.

WEEK 46: GUARDING YOUR FAMILY IN A DIGITAL WORLD

GOD'S TRUTH

"Above all else, guard your heart, for everything you do flows from it."–Proverbs 4:23 (ESV)

DEVOTIONAL THOUGHT

The threats to your family used to knock at the front door. Now they slip in through screens in every pocket. The digital world offers incredible opportunities and terrifying dangers, often simultaneously. Your children navigate spaces you can't always see, facing temptations you never imagined at their age.

Guarding your family digitally isn't just about screen time limits and content filters—though those matter. It's about teaching them to guard their own hearts. Every app, game, and platform is shaping their minds and souls. The question isn't whether they'll encounter darkness online, but whether they'll know what to do when they do.

This requires more conversation than restriction. When you only build walls without explaining why, they'll eventually climb over them. But when you teach them to recognize danger, evaluate content through God's truth, and flee from spiritual harm, you're equipping them for a lifetime of digital decisions.

Your own digital habits preach loudly. When they see you scrolling endlessly, choosing screens over family, or consuming questionable content, your rules ring hollow. Guard your own heart first. Create a family culture where real relationships matter more than virtual ones, where God's truth filters what enters your home through any door—physical or digital.

A PRAYER FOR YOU

Father, the digital world feels overwhelming and dangerous. Give me wisdom to guard my family without just building walls of fear. Help me model healthy digital habits. Protect my children from online dangers while teaching them to guard their own hearts. Guide us through this digital age. Amen.

YOUR CHALLENGE

This week, initiate an honest family conversation about digital challenges. Share your own struggles with technology. Create one family agreement about digital use—maybe no phones at dinner or devices charge outside bedrooms. Make it collaborative, not dictatorial.

TAKE A MOMENT

Consider what your current digital habits are teaching your children. Ask God to reveal any areas where you need to model better boundaries with technology. Your example matters more than your rules.

WEEK 47: FAITHFUL LEADERSHIP AT HOME

GOD'S TRUTH

"He must manage his own household well, with all dignity keeping his children submissive, for if someone does not know how to manage his own household, how will he care for God's church?"–1 Timothy 3:4-5 (ESV)

DEVOTIONAL THOUGHT

Leadership at home doesn't mean ruling with an iron fist. It means creating an environment where God's ways are normal, where faith is practical, and where each family member can flourish under your protective guidance. You're not just managing a household—you're shepherding hearts.

Faithful leadership starts with your own walk with God. Your family can't follow you somewhere you're not going. When they see you consistently seeking God, submitting to His Word, and serving others, they understand what spiritual leadership looks like. Your life preaches the sermon they'll remember.

This leadership requires consistency between Sunday and Monday. If faith only shows up at church, your children learn that God is compartmentalized, not integrated. But when biblical principles guide family decisions, conflicts, and celebrations, faith becomes the foundation, not just decoration.

Managing your household well doesn't mean perfection—it means direction. It means everyone knows this family serves the Lord. It means grace covers failures, but standards still matter. It means Dad leads with love, not intimidation. Your home is your first ministry. How you lead there determines your credibility everywhere else. When you're faithful in the small kingdom of your home, God can trust you with more.

A PRAYER FOR YOU

Lord, help me lead my household with faithful consistency. Show me how to shepherd my family's hearts toward You. Give me wisdom to lead with love and strength. Make our home a place where Your ways are celebrated and followed. Help me be faithful in this first ministry. Amen.

YOUR CHALLENGE

This week, evaluate one area of family life that needs stronger leadership—maybe it's spiritual disciplines, conflict resolution, or family priorities. Take one concrete step to provide direction in that area. Lead by example first, then bring others along.

TAKE A MOMENT

Consider what kind of spiritual culture exists in your home. Is faith integrated into daily life or relegated to Sundays? Ask God for one practical way to strengthen faithful leadership in your household today.

WEEK 48: BLESSING YOUR FAMILY WITH YOUR WORDS

GOD'S TRUTH

"Let no corrupting talk come out of your mouths, but only such as is good for building up, as fits the occasion, that it may give grace to those who hear."–Ephesians 4:29 (ESV)

DEVOTIONAL THOUGHT

Your words carry more weight than you realize. A father's voice has unique power to bless or wound, to build up or tear down. Years from now, your children will still hear your words echoing in their minds. What will that internal soundtrack say?

Blessing isn't just saying nice things—it's speaking God's truth over your family. It's calling out the gold in them before it's fully visible. It's declaring God's promises over their struggles. When you speak blessing, you're agreeing with heaven about who they are and who they're becoming.

This means being intentional with your words. Instead of "you always" or "you never," speak hope: "I see growth in you." Replace criticism with vision: "God is developing something special in you." Transform correction into blessing: "You're better than this behavior."

Your children are desperate for Dad's blessing. They need to hear you're proud of them, that you believe in them, that you see God working in them. Your wife needs words that build her up after the world tears her down. Every word is either a brick building them up or a hammer tearing them down. Choose construction over demolition. Your words today become their inner voice tomorrow.

A PRAYER FOR YOU

Father, forgive me for careless words that have wounded rather than blessed. Set a guard over my mouth. Fill it with words that build up and give grace. Help me speak blessing over my family daily. Let my words echo Your love and truth in their hearts forever. Amen.

YOUR CHALLENGE

This week, speak a specific blessing over each family member every day. Not generic praise, but targeted truth about their identity and future. Do it at bedtime, breakfast, or whenever you can look them in the eye and speak life into their soul.

TAKE A MOMENT

Think about the most powerful words of blessing someone ever spoke over you. Feel their lasting impact. Now determine to give that same gift to your family through intentional, life-giving words.

WEEK 49: LOOKING BACK: HOW FAR YOU'VE COME

GOD'S TRUTH

"I thank my God in all my remembrance of you, always in every prayer of mine for you all making my prayer with joy, because of your partnership in the gospel from the first day until now."–Philippians 1:3-5 (ESV)

DEVOTIONAL THOUGHT

Pause for a moment and look back. Remember that terrified new father holding his first child? Remember the mistakes you were certain would ruin them? Remember the nights you had no idea what you were doing? Look how far God has brought you.

You're not the same father you were last year, let alone when you started. Every prayer prayed, every lesson learned through failure, every moment you chose love over anger— it's all been building something. You've grown. They've grown. Your family has traveled miles together, even when it felt like standing still.

Looking back isn't about living in the past—it's about recognizing God's faithfulness. That crisis you thought would break your family? You survived it. That child you worried would never change? See their growth. That marriage that felt hopeless? Still standing. God has been writing a story of grace.

Your journey as a father is a partnership with God. He's been there through every victory and defeat, working all things together for good. The father you are today stands on the foundation of every yesterday. Thank God for the journey—the struggles that strengthened you, the joys that sustained you, the grace that carried you. You've come farther than you realize.

A PRAYER FOR YOU

Father, thank You for the journey You've brought me on as a dad. I see Your faithfulness in every season, Your grace in every failure, Your strength in every challenge. Thank You for not giving up on me. Help me see how far we've come and trust You with how far we still need to go. Amen.

YOUR CHALLENGE

This week, share with your family three specific ways you've seen God's faithfulness in your journey together. Celebrate growth—yours and theirs. Create a moment of remembrance and gratitude for how far God has brought your family.

TAKE A MOMENT

Flip through old photos of your family. See the passage of time, the growth, the journey. Thank God for every season He's brought you through. Let gratitude for the past strengthen faith for the future.

WEEK 50: LIVING INTENTIONALLY AS A DAD

GOD'S TRUTH

"So teach us to number our days that we may get a heart of wisdom." — Psalm 90:12 (ESV)

DEVOTIONAL THOUGHT

Fatherhood can feel like survival mode—just making it through each day. But what if you shifted from reactive to intentional? What if every interaction, decision, and moment was filtered through the question: "How is this shaping my child's future?"

Intentional fatherhood means having a vision for each child and daily decisions that serve that vision. It means knowing what values you're building and what legacy you're leaving. It's choosing presence over presents, relationships over achievements, and eternal over temporary.

Living intentionally requires saying no to good things to say yes to best things. That extra project at work might be good, but your son's game might be best. That hobby might be relaxing, but family time might be more important. Every yes is a no to something else—choose wisely.

The days are evil, full of distractions designed to steal your focus from what matters most. Your phone, career, and entertainments all compete for attention that belongs to your family. Intentional fathers recognize these thieves and guard their time fiercely. You have approximately 936 weeks from birth until they turn eighteen. How many have already passed? Make the remaining ones count. Live with purpose, parent with intention, and lead with eternity in mind.

A PRAYER FOR YOU

Lord, help me stop drifting through fatherhood and start living intentionally. Give me vision for each child and wisdom to make daily decisions that serve that vision. Help me recognize time-stealers and choose what matters most. Make every remaining day count for eternity. Amen.

YOUR CHALLENGE

This week, write a one-sentence vision for each child—who you hope they become in Christ. Then evaluate your current schedule and choices. Do they serve these visions? Make one change that reflects more intentional fatherhood.

TAKE A MOMENT

Calculate roughly how many weeks remain until each child turns eighteen. Let that number motivate intentional choices. Time is limited, but it's not too late to make the most of what remains.

WEEK 51: PREPARING YOUR FAMILY FOR TOMORROW

GOD'S TRUTH

"Prepare your work outside; get everything ready for yourself in the field, and after that build your house."–Proverbs 24:27 (ESV)

DEVOTIONAL THOUGHT

You're not just managing today—you're preparing them for all their tomorrows. Every lesson taught, every skill developed, every truth planted is equipping them for a future you won't always be part of. This reality should shape every decision you make today.

Preparing your family for tomorrow means more than college funds and life insurance. It means building character that will sustain them through trials. It means establishing faith that will anchor them in storms. It means creating memories that will comfort them when you're gone.

What do they need to know? How to hear God's voice when Dad's not around to give advice. How to handle money when there's no one checking their spending. How to choose a spouse, raise children, and navigate life's complexities. These preparations happen in today's ordinary moments.

You're writing a manual they'll reference long after you're gone. Every time you handle conflict with grace, they're learning relationship skills. When you manage money wisely, they're absorbing financial wisdom. When you prioritize

God, they're understanding what matters most. Your today is preparing their tomorrow. Make sure you're equipping them for a future where faith, character, and wisdom matter more than any inheritance you could leave.

A PRAYER FOR YOU

Father, help me see today's parenting through tomorrow's lens. Show me what my children need to know for the future they'll face. Give me wisdom to prepare them practically and spiritually for life beyond my home. Help me equip them for every good work You have planned. Amen.

YOUR CHALLENGE

This week, teach each child one practical life skill they'll need—maybe cooking a meal, changing a tire, or managing money. More importantly, share the biblical principle behind the skill. Prepare them for tomorrow by being intentional today.

TAKE A MOMENT

Imagine your children as adults facing life's challenges. What do you hope you will have equipped them with? Let that vision guide your preparation efforts today.

WEEK 52: WALKING BOLDLY IN GOD'S PLANS

GOD'S TRUTH

"Have I not commanded you? Be strong and courageous. Do not be frightened, and do not be dismayed, for the Lord your God is with you wherever you go."–Joshua 1:9 (ESV)

DEVOTIONAL THOUGHT

You've made it through 52 weeks of seeking God's heart for fatherhood. You've faced hard truths, embraced challenges, and grown in ways you couldn't have imagined. But this isn't an ending—it's a commissioning. God has plans for your family that require bold faith.

Walking boldly doesn't mean having everything figured out. It means stepping forward even when the path isn't clear, trusting the One who guides your steps. It means making decisions based on faith, not fear. It means leading your family into God's purposes even when it's uncomfortable.

God's plans for your family are bigger than your imagination. That child you're raising might impact nations. The faith you're building could ripple through generations. The love you're modeling is shaping future families. You're part of something eternal, something magnificent.

Don't shrink back now. Don't let fear keep you from God's best for your family. He who commanded Joshua commands you: Be strong and courageous. The Lord your God is with you—in every parenting decision, through every family crisis, for every step forward. Walk boldly, Dad. Heaven is backing you, your family is following you, and God's plans are waiting for you. This is your moment to lead with confident faith into everything God has prepared.

A PRAYER FOR YOU

Father, thank You for this journey of growth as a father. Now give me boldness to walk in Your plans for my family. Remove fear and fill me with courage. Help me lead with confident faith into the future You've prepared. I trust You with my family's destiny. We're Yours. Amen.

YOUR CHALLENGE

This week, take one bold step of faith for your family—maybe it's a decision you've been postponing, a conversation you've been avoiding, or a change you know God's calling you to make. Step out in courage, trusting God with the results.

TAKE A MOMENT

Stand up right now. Literally stand and declare out loud: "As for me and my house, we will serve the Lord." Feel the weight and privilege of that declaration. Walk boldly in that truth, knowing God goes with you.

DISCOVER MORE BOOKS

Start each day with purpose, peace, and a deeper connection to God. Whether you're nurturing your own faith, guiding your children, or growing together as a family—this devotional series meets you right where life happens.

Collect the Whole Series

Devotional for Dads

Devotional for Moms

Devotional for Kids

Available at major online bookstores

Each book is a spiritual companion—designed to inspire, uplift, and transform. Together, they form a complete journey of faith for the whole family.

Don't wait—bring home the full set and let every day draw you closer to God, to each other, and to the life you were created for.